A Kid's Guide

England

Curious Kids Press • Palm Springs, CA

www.curiouskidspress.com

info@curiouskids press.com

Publisher: *Curious Kids Press, Palm Springs, CA 92264.*
Designed by: Michael Owens
Editor: *Sterling Moss*
Copy Editor: *Janice Ross*

Photo: Painting of Saint George, the patron saint of England

Table of Contents

3

Welcome to England

WHAT DO YOU THINK OF FIRST when you think about England? Buckingham Palace? Big Ben? The Hogwarts School of Witchcraft and Wizardry?

All of these places are part of what makes England fun and interesting. And in this book about this history-rich country, you'll learn more about all of those fascinating places.

But there is much more to see and learn about England– from the Tower of London and the Legend of the Ravens to the British Royal Family, of course. So, let's get started on this adventure to England.

Background Photo: Trafalgar Square in the heart of London and Nelson's Column

Your Passport to England

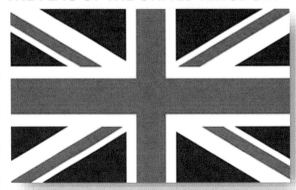

Official Name: England
Location: Great Britain
Capital City: London
Country Area (Size): 50,302 sq. mi (130,282 sq. km) About the size of Alabama.
Population: 53,012,456 (2011 census)
Official Language: English
Currency: British pound

THE FLAG OF THE UNITED KINGDOM

THE FLAG OF THE UNITED KINGDOM, which includes England, Scotland, Wales, and Northern Ireland, is known as the Union Jack. It combines the following symbols:

- England's patron saint, St. George (red cross on a white background)

- Scotland's patron saint, St. Andrew (diagonal white cross on blue), and

- Ireland's patron saint, San Patricio (diagonal red cross on white).

(Wales is not shown on the flag of the United Kingdom because when the first version of the flag was created in 1606 Wales was part of England, not a separate country.)

THE FLAG OF ENGLAND features a solid red cross on a white background. The red cross is called Saint George's Cross. It represents Saint George, who was a Roman solider and priest nearly two thousand years ago.

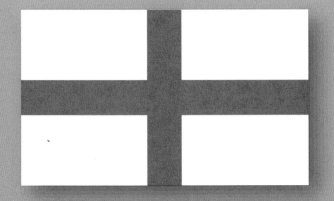

Where in the World Is England?

Did You Know?

You can use the term "Britain" to mean the island of Great Britain or the country of the United Kingdom.

ENGLAND IS PART OF THE UNITED KINGDOM of Great Britain and Northern Ireland. (It is often called just the UK or sometimes "Britain.")

England is on the island of Great Britain, the 9th largest island in the world. It is bordered by Wales to the west and Scotland to the north. Both Wales and Scotland are also part of the island of Great Britain and the United Kingdom.

England is separated from continental Europe by the North Sea to the east and the English Channel to the south.

A Brief History of England

43 AD: Roman emperor Claudius conquers what is now Britain.

501–600: German peoples move into Britain; the English become known as the Anglo-Saxons.

1066 AD: France's William, Duke of Normandy, defeats the Anglo-Saxon king at the Battle of Hastings and becomes King.

1346 -1353: London loses at least half of it population during the Black Death, one of he most devastating diseases in human history.

1485: Henry Tudor, a Welsh nobleman, claims the English crown and becomes Henry VII, the first of five Tudor monarchs.

1534: Henry VIII breaks away from the Roman Catholic Church. He declares himself the Supreme Head of the Church of England.

1620: Pilgrims set sale on the Mayflower for the New World.

1760: George III becomes King of Great Britain and Ireland. He opposes independence for the American colonies during the American Revolutionary War.

1776: American colonies formally declare independence from England.

1837: Victoria becomes Queen of the United Kingdom of Great Britain and Ireland at the age of 18. She reigns until 1901.

1939-1945: Prime Minister Winston Churchill leads the British to victory against Germany, Japan, and Italy in World War II.

1952: Elizabeth Mary Alexandra becomes Queen Elizabeth II.

1979: Margaret Thatcher becomes Britain's first woman Prime Minister.

2011: Prince William, son of Prince Charles and Diana, Princess of Wales, and the future King of England, marries Catherine Middleton in Westminster Abbey.

Famous Cities in England

ENGLAND IS DIVIDED into nine regions. Each region has many fascinating and fun cities to visit. Here are some famous cities in those regions and what each city is known for.

District: North East
NEWCASTLE UPON TYNE
Famous For: The Blinking Eye Bridge

District: Yorkshire and the Humber
YORK
Famous For: Chocolate (for over 300 years).

District: North West
LIVERPOOL
Famous For: The Beatles

District: East Midlands
NOTTINGHAM
Famous For: Sherwood Forest

District: West Midlands
STRATFORD-ON-AVON
Famous For: Birthplace of William Shakespeare

District: East Angila
CAMBRIDGE
Famous For: The University of Cambridge

District: Greater London
LONDON

District: South West
BATH
Famous For: Roman Baths

District: South East
OXFORD
Famous For: Oxford University

How to Speak British English

Do you speak English? Maybe not the way it's spoken in England. Let's see how good you are at understanding British English. Look at the words in the speech balloons. In the box below each word, write what you think the "American English" word is. (Answers on page 35.)

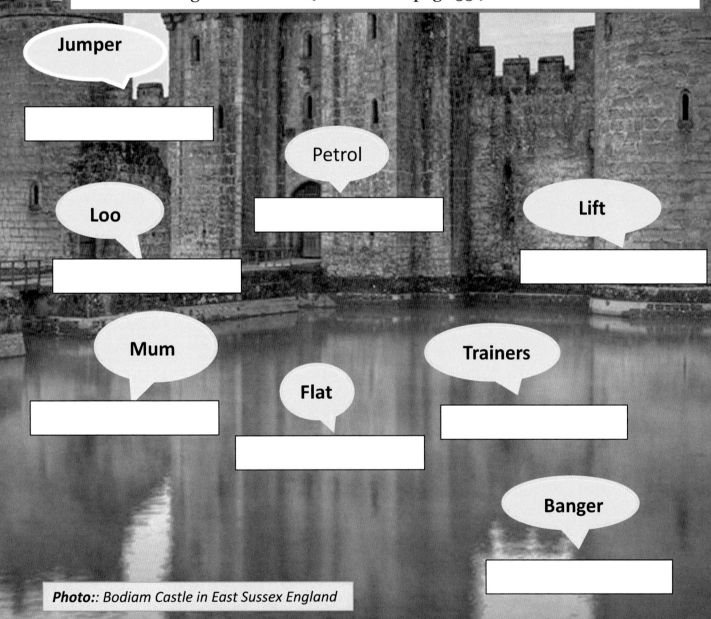

Jumper

Petrol

Loo

Lift

Mum

Trainers

Flat

Banger

Photo:: Bodiam Castle in East Sussex England

Fun Facts About England

George I, who reigned from 1714 to 1727, could speak only a few words of English.

There are 760 windows (give or take) in Buckingham Palace, the home of the British **monarch**. They are cleaned every six weeks.

J.K. Rowling, author of the Harry Potter books, was born in Yate, Gloucestershire, England. She is the first author ever to become a billionaire. BTW, J.K. stands for Joanne Kathleen.

French was the official language of England from 1066 to 1362.

The Thames River is the longest river in England. It's 215 miles (346 km) long.

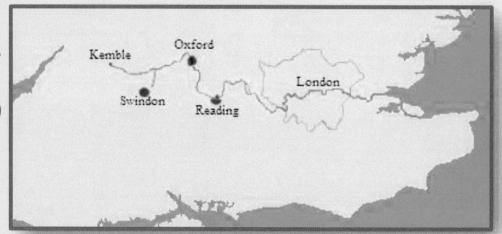

Kemble Oxford London Swindon Reading

Each year, more than 2.5 million people visit the Tower of London where the Crown Jewels are kept in a vault.

Windsor Castle is the oldest and largest royal residence still in use in the world.

The island of Great Britain is the 9th largest island in the world. It is also the most populous.

No one who lives in England is more than 75 miles (120 km) from the sea.

Oxford University is the world's oldest English-speaking university.

More than 1 million people visit Buckingham Palace every year.

Twenty-four bridges span the River Thames. The oldest is London Bridge which was first built by the Roman founders of London. The current London Bridge opened in 1973.

Drawing of the way London Bridge looked in 1682.

Famous Places in ENGLAND

Buckingham Palace

BUCKINGHAM PALACE is the official home of the British monarch (king or queen). And what a home it is. There are more than 775 rooms, 78 bathrooms, and 300 fireplaces.

In some ways, Buckingham Palace (including the palace gardens) is like a little town. It has its own chapel, its own post office, its own movie theater, its own swimming pool, and its own tennis courts. It also has a boating lake and a helicopter landing pad.

George III bought Buckingham Palace in 1761 for 21,000 pounds. That's about $27,000. How much do you think it's worth today?

Fun Fact

There are more than 450 clocks in the Palace. Every year it takes the Queen's clock maker 16 hours to move the clocks forward by one hour for British Summer Time. (We call it Daylight Saving Time.) Come October, he has to move them all back one hour.

Changing the Guard

EVERY MORNING AT BUCKINGHAM PALACE, there is an important and colorful ceremony. It's called Changing the Guard (or, officially, Guard Mounting). That is when the "Old Guard" (the soldiers currently on duty) hands over responsibility for guarding the Palace to the "New Guard." A band provides a variety of music during the ceremony, which lasts about 45 minute.

Five regiments of the British Army form the Queen's Foot Guards (or King's Foot Guards when the monarch is a male). The guards stand at attention in front of their **sentry box**, not moving a muscle. But every 10 minutes or so they turn and march back and forth in front of their sentry box.

What happens if someone steps in front of the guard as he marches back and forth? The guard will shout "Make way for the Queen's Guard." With that , people usually move out of the way.

The Queen's Guard is a very special group of soldiers. They have been guarding the King or Queen of England for more than 500 years.

What They Wear

It's hard to miss the Queen's foot guards. They definitely stand out in a crowd. They wear a deep red jacket (or tunic) and black bearskin (a tall fur cap).

London Eye

Inside one of the capsules on the London Eye.

https://de.wikipedia.org/wiki/User:Swgreed

THE LONDON EYE (aka **Millennium** Wheel) is a giant Ferris wheel on the River Thames. It was built in 1999. At the time it was the tallest Ferris Wheel in the world.

The **diameter** is 394 ft (120 m). That's wider than a football field.

The wheel has 32 capsules. Each one hold up to 25 people, who can walk around in the capsule.

World's Tallest Ferris Wheels

1999: **London Eye**: 443 ft (135 m)

2006: Star of Nanchang (China)**:** 520 ft (158 m)

2008 Singapore Flyer: 541 ft. (165 m)

2014 High Roller (Las Vegas): 550 ft (168 m).

Hadrian's Wall

CHINA HAS "THE GREAT WALL," but England has a famous wall, too. It's called Hadrian's Wall.

The coast-to-coast wall (from the North Sea across England to the Irish Sea) was built by the Roman Emperor Hadrian. He began construction of the wall in 122 AD. He wanted to protect Roman England from the tribes who lived in Scotland. He also wanted to mark where the Roman Empire ended.

When it was built, it was 73 miles (117.5 km) long. It also was as much as 15 ft. (4.5 m) tall. Even though it is more than 2,000 years old, parts of Hadrian's Wall still exist today.

Did You Know? Hadrian's Wall was more than just a stone wall. Along the way, there were milecastles – small, rectangular forts. These were built about one Roman mile apart along the wall. There were also numerous observation towers (or turrets) as well as 17 larger forts.

Big Ben

Attribution: DS Pugh

ONE OF THE MOST POPULAR tourist attractions in London (or all of England for that matter) is Big Ben. What makes it so special? The tower is home to a 13-ton bell.

The clock tower itself is often called Big Ben. But that name actually belongs to the bell. It got its name from the man who first ordered the bell, Sir Benjamin (Ben) Hall.

Big Ben stands 315 feet high (96 m) tall. That's more than twice as tall as the Statue of Liberty.

The bell itself is about 7 feet (2.2 m) tall. It took nearly 13 years to build. It was first chimed in July 1859. Today, it rings every 15 minutes.

More recently, the tower was renamed to Elizabeth Tower to honor Queen Elizabeth II.

> **Did You Know?** The minute hand on the clock in Big Ben weighs 220 pounds and is just over 12 feet long.

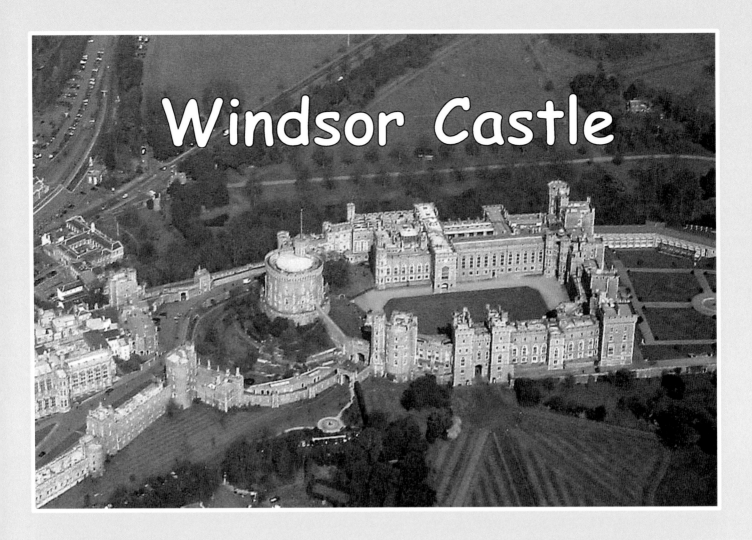

Windsor Castle

CASTLES ARE FUN, no matter where they are. And in England, Windsor Castle is a blast. It's Queen Elizabeth's second home. (Buckingham Palace is her main home, which is about 22 miles (35 km) away.)

Windsor Castle has everything a castle should have. There's a moat, turrets, a real drawbridge. And, since this is the Queen's home, there are the Queen's guards.

Windsor Castle is not a single building. It is a large complex of buildings that form a nearly rectangular wall on 13 acres (5.3 ha).

Within the complex there are two courtyards known as the upper and lower wards. They are separated by a massive Round Tower in the middle ward that separates the two sets of buildings.

The original castle was built by William the Conqueror in the 11th century. Today, more than 500 people (not counting the Queen) live and work in Windsor Castle.

Stonehenge
A Mysterious Monument

STONEHENGE IS ONE OF THE MOST IMPORTANT prehistoric sites in the world. It's located near the town Amesbury, which is about 83 miles (134 km) from London.

Stonehenge consists of a ring of standing stones. Each stone is about 13 ft (4.1 m) tall and nearly 7 ft (2.1 m) wide and weighs around 25 tons.

Stonehenge is said to be more than 5,000 years old. It was constructed sometime between 3000 BC to 2000 BC.

The stones had to be moved 240 miles (385 km) from the place where they were mined. No one has yet figured out how they were moved that far.

Nobody knows for sure who built the monument – or why. Some **archaeologists** believe it might have been a cemetery.

The Channel Tunnel (AKA Chunnel)

WHAT'S THE BEST WAY to get from England to France? You can fly, of course. Or you could take the Channel Tunnel.

The Channel Tunnel is a 31-mile (50-km) rail tunnel beneath the English Channel. It carries both passenger trains and the Eurotunnel Shuttle for cars.

It was officially opened on May 6, 1994. Today, it takes 35 minutes to travel across the Channel Tunnel from England to France. The flying time from London to Paris is about 55 minutes.

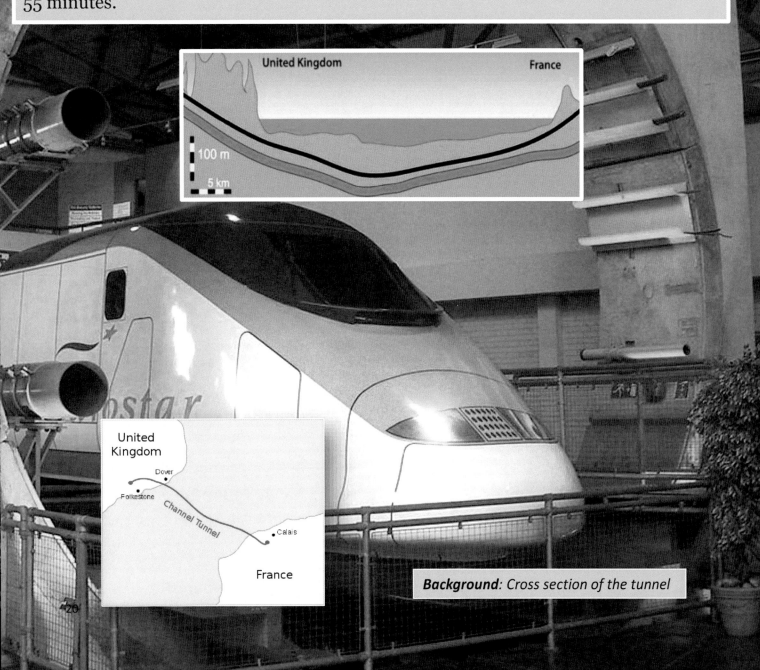

Background: Cross section of the tunnel

The Blinking Eye Bridge
(The Coolest Bridge in the World)

THE GATESHEAD MILLENNIUM BRIDGE (better known as "The Blinking Eye" bridge) is a **pedestrian** bridge that spans the River Tyne. It opens (tilts sideways) to let river traffic to pass underneath. The bridge made its debut on June 20, 2001. More than 36,000 people stood on the banks of the River Tyne to watch the bridge tilt for the first time. The bridge connects Newcastle on the north side of the River Tyne with Gateshead on the south.

To watch the bridge tilt, copy and paste this link in your URL:
https://www.youtube.com/watch?v=dkjY6COhR0QK

The Tube
The World's First Underground Railway

Then...

And now.

Photo: tompagenet (Tom Page)

THE WORLD'S FIRST UNDERGROUND RAILWAY opened in London in 1863. It provided service between Paddington and Farringdon, a distance of about 3.8 miles (6.1 km). The system back then used gas-lit wooden carriages pulled by steam locomotives.

Today, the system has 250 miles (400 km) of track and 270 stations. The deepest station is 192 ft (58.5 m) below ground. The longest trip on one train is about 34 miles (54.5 km). The shortest trip between two stations is 853 ft. (260 m). The trip takes 20 seconds.

There's one other interesting fact about the underground railway. More than half of the system is not actually underground at all!

During World War II, 79 tube stations were used as air raid shelters by Londoners.

> **FOR HARRY POTTER FANS ONLY:**
> What character has a scar on his knee shaped just like the London Underground map? Check your answer on page 35.

The Tower of London

ENTRY TO THE TRAITORS GATE

THE NAME – THE TOWER OF LONDON -- sounds like it is one tall monument, doesn't it?

But the Tower of London is actually a 900-year-old palace (and fortress) consisting of several buildings located within two concentric rings of walls on over 12 acres (5 hectares). Construction was started by William the Conqueror in 1078.

The castle has been used for many different things, including a royal palace and a prison. During the 1500s, many executions and beheadings took place in the Tower of London, including two of King Henry VIII's ex-wives.

Today, it is home to the Crown Jewels. The jewels include the crowns worn by the monarch at coronation and at the opening of Parliament. But the crown jewels include more than just **sovereign** crowns. (There are seven of those.) There are also swords, scepters, robes, rings, and many other items – 141 in all.

The Tower of London
The Legend of the Raven

FOR MORE THAN 350 YEARS, six magnificent black birds, known as ravens, have occupied the Tower of London. (Not the same ones all that time, of course.) Legend has it that if these six ravens ever leave the fortress, the White Tower will crumble and a great disaster will befall all of England.

So just to be on the safe side, this group of crow-like birds lead a rather cushy life at the Tower, cared for by the Raven Master.

He makes sure the ravens get enough meat to eat – at least 8 ounces every day – as well as "bird biscuits soaked in blood." Ugh! The Raven Master says they also love cheese.

Sports in England

CAN YOU GUESS what the three most favorite team sports are in England? It probably won't come as a surprise that the number one favorite is soccer (or as they call it in England, football). But the other two most favorite team sports are not very common in the U.S. One is cricket and the other is rugby.

Cricket is the unofficial national sport of the United Kingdom, just like baseball is the unofficial sport in the United States. Cricket is also similar to baseball. It is a bat-and-ball game played between two teams of eleven players. But there are also some significant differences.

Cricket

Rugby

Rugby is the third most favorite team sport in England. It's sort of like American football. One big difference is that a rugby league match lasts 80 minutes. A football game can last much longer. One other difference is that rugby players don't wear nearly as much protective gear as American football players.

Bumps Race

A popular sports competition held every year at the University of Cambridge and the University of Oxford is called the bumps race. It's a type of rowing race in which a number of boats chase each other in a single file and try to, well, bump the boat in front of them out of the race.

The start of a bump race.

Wimbledon

Wimbledon is a district in England. It's about 7 miles (11.3 km) from the center of London.

But it is also the location of the oldest and probably best known tennis tournament in the world.

The Wimbledon tennis tournament is one of only four tennis Grand Slam events held each year and the only one to be played on grass courts.

Centre court at Wimbledon

Did You Know? In 2013, Wimbledon champ Roger Federer was told to change his shoes. Can you guess why? Find out on page 35.

Three Famous British Monarchs

ON MAY 1, 1707, THE KINGDOM OF ENGLAND and the Kingdom of Scotland joined together (or merged). Together, they formed the Kingdom of Great Britain.

One hundred years later, in 1801, Great Britain merged with the Kingdom of Ireland and the country became the United Kingdom of Great Britain and Ireland.

Finally, in 1922, the southern part of Ireland left the union. The United Kingdom became known as it is today – The United Kingdom of Great Britain and Northern Ireland.

Since 1707, there have been 12 **monarchs** (kings and queens). Here are three of them. Read more about each of these famous monarchs on the next three pages.

King Henry VIII at age 18

Queen Victoria at her coronation in 1838.

Queen Elizabeth II at her coronation in 1953..

Did You Know? Today, the government of the UK is a **constitutional monarchy**. In this form of government, there is a monarch and a prime minister.

A monarch (king or queen) is the head of state, but doesn't have any real political power.

The prime minister is the head of the government. He or she manages the politics of a country and is a member of the **Parliament**.

The Parliament makes all the country's laws.

KING HENRY VIII was one of the most interesting kings in the history of England. As a young man he was a great athlete. He spoke five languages. He was also a good musician.

He became king at the age of 17 and ruled for nearly 40 years. During that time, he accomplished many things that were good for the country.

But Henry also had quite a few flaws. He married six times, and had two of his wives executed. He split from the Catholic Church and made himself head of the Church of England. If anyone refused to accept him as head of the church, he would have that person executed.

THE SIX WIVES OF HENRY VIII

1. Catherine of Aragon
Married: 1509-1533
Divorced

2. Anne Boleyn
Married: 1533 - 1536
Executed

3. Jane Seymour
Married: 1536 - 1537
Died

4. Anne of Cleves
Married: Jan-July 1540
Marriage Annulled

5. Kathryn Howard
Married: 1540 - 1542
Executed

6. Katherine Parr
Married: 1543 - 1547
Outlived Henry

Queen Victoria
Her Reign: 1837 - 1901

UNTIL ELIZABETH II, Queen Victoria ruled longer than any other British monarch in history. She was Queen of the United Kingdom of Great Britain and Ireland and later also Empress of India.

When she became queen at the age of 18, many people thought she would be a weak monarch and not accomplish much. But during her reign, Britain became the richest and most powerful country in the world.

Victoria's husband died when she was only 42 years old. For the rest of her life, she wore black in public.

During her reign, there were at least seven attempts to assassinate (or to kill) her. But she survived them all .

Fun Fact 1:
Grandmother of Europe

Victoria had nine children who married royalty or nobles throughout Europe and gave her 40 grandchildren. As a result, she got the nickname "Grandmother of Europe."

Fun Fact 2
Happy Wedding

Victoria proposed to her future husband, Albert. (Since she was Queen, he wasn't allowed to propose to her.) She also started the tradition of wearing a white wedding dress.

Fun Fact 3
Long Live the Queen

During her reign, 10 different men served as President of the United States – from Martin Van Buren, the 8th president of the United States to William McKinley, the 17th American president.

Queen Elizabeth II
Her Reign: 1952 - Present

Queen Elizabeth II

IN 1952, 25-YEAR OLD ELIZABETH MARY ALEXANDRA became Queen Elizabeth II, Queen of the United Kingdom, Canada, Australia, and New Zealand.

To a certain extent, she became queen almost by accident. When she was a young girl, her uncle was King. His name was Edward VIII. But in 1936, Edward VIII **abdicated**.

As a result, Edward VIII's brother – and Elizabeth's father – became King. His name was King George VI.

King George had two daughters – Elizabeth and Margaret. Elizabeth was the older daughter. So when King George VI died, Elizabeth became Queen Elizabeth II.

On September 9, 2015, Queen Elizabeth II became the longest ruling monarch in British history. She was 89 years old at the time.

Two years later, she celebrated her Sapphire Jubilee, marking 65 years on the throne. She is the only British monarch to ever celebrate a Sapphire Jubilee.

Did You Know? Queen Elizabeth II became Queen in February 1952 when her father died. But her **coronation** didn't take place until more than a year later, on June 2, 1953.

Who Will Become King (or Queen)

Queen Elizabeth, II

IN THE UNITED STATES, if the President dies or resigns (quits) while in office, the Vice President becomes President for the rest of the term. That's an example of the Presidential line of **succession** – the order in which government officials assume the presidency if the President dies, resigns, or is removed from office.

In Great Britain, there is also a line of succession. Follow the current line of succession in this flow-chart.

Her son, Charles, Prince of Wales

His son Prince William, Duke of Cambridge

His son Prince George

Did You Know? It used to be that males would always come before females in the line of succession to the throne – even if the female was older than the male. That all changed in 2015. Now the line of succession is determined by age – older first, no matter if it's male or female.

Kate Middleton
A Future Queen Consort*

SHE'S PROBABLY ONE OF THE MOST POPULAR ROYALS in all of the United Kingdom and maybe even all of Europe. She was born Catherine (Kate) Middleton. But today she is known as Catherine, Duchess of Cambridge.

On April 29, 2011, Kate Middleton, a commoner (or person without rank or title), married Prince William, Duke of Cambridge. William is the grandson of Queen Elizabeth II and future King. That makes Kate a future queen consort.

As of 2022, William and Kate have three children – Prince George of Cambridge (born July 2013), Princess Charlotte of Cambridge (born May 2015), and Prince Louis of Cambridge (born April 2018). They are all in line to the British throne.

Photo: William and Kate in Ottawa, July 2011

Did You Know? Kate met her prince when they were both students at the University of Saint Andrews in Scotland in 2001.

* **Queen Consort**: A queen consort is the wife of a reigning king. She usually shares her spouse's social rank and status, but does not formally share political and military powers.

Harry Potter's England

Do Diagon Alley, the Knight Bus bridge, or Platform 9 $\frac{3}{4}$ at King's Cross train station mean anything to you? If so, then you must be a Harry Potter fan. And what better place to follow in the footsteps of Harry Potter and friends than in England, where much of the movie magic was filmed. Here are some of the places you might recognize from the movies.

The Movie: Diagon Alley and the Leaky Cauldron Pub.

Real Life: Leadenhall Market is a covered market in London. It was built in 1881. It was used to represent the area around Diagon Alley and the Leaky Cauldron.

Attribution: Photo by DAVID ILIFF. License: CC-BY-SA 3.0

The Movie: King's Cross Station, where students board the Hogwarts Express from the hidden Platform 9 3/4.

Real Life: The real King's Cross Railway station is more than 150 years old. It's on the northern edge of London. Today, at the station, you can find the hidden access to Platform 9 $\frac{3}{4}$.

Photo: Cmglee - Own work

The Movie: Hogsmeade Station: This is the end of the line for the Hogwarts Express in Harry Potter films. It's where students disembark for Hogwarts School.

Real Life: In real life, Hogsmeade Station is really Goathland railway station, the station for the village of Goathland near Grosmont, North Yorkshire, England.

The Movie: Hogwarts School of Witchcraft and Wizardry. Also the Quidditch scenes.

Real Life: Alnwick Castle at Alnwick, Northumberland. Part of the castle is still used today as a private residence.

The Movie: Remember when Harry first learned he could talk to snakes?

Real Life: It was filmed at London Zoo's Reptile House, home to more than 650 species.

The Movie: The cloister walk in Harry Potter and the Chamber of Secrets

Real Life: The scene was filmed at Lacock Abbey in the village of Lacock, Wiltshire, England.

Glossary

Abdicate To give up something, such as a throne or power or responsibility.

Archaeologist A scientist who studies past human life and culture.

British Isles A group of islands that consist of Great Britain, Ireland, and more than 6,000 smaller isles off the north-western coast of Europe.

Constitutional Monarchy A system of government in which the powers of the monarch (or ruler) are restricted by the constitution and the laws of the nation.

Coronation A ceremony in which a monarch (or ruler) is crowned.

Diameter The length of a line passing through the center of a circle or sphere and has its end on either side of the circle or sphere.

Millennium A unit of time equal to one thousand years.

Monarch A sole ruler, such as a king or queen, whose position is usually hereditary or passed on from a parent.

Parliament A national lawmaking body consisting of elected representative. The UK Parliament consists of the House of Commons and House of Lords.

Pedestrian A person who is walking.

Reign (noun) The period of a particular monarch's rule.

Sentry Box A small shelter in which a guard may stand to be sheltered from the weather.

Sovereign A monarch or other royal ruler.

Succession The act of following or coming after in sequence.

We hope you enjoyed reading this book about our country.

Come visit us sometime.

"How to Speak British English" answers

Banger - sausage

Jumper - sweater

Loo - toilet

Lift - elevator

Trainers - sneakers

Petrol - gas

Mum - mother

Flat - apartment

So why was Roger Federer told to change his shoes at a match at Wimbledon? Wimbledon has a strict dress code. Players must be dressed almost entirely in white. In 2013 Roger Federer had to change his shoes because the soles of the shoes were orange!

FOR HARRY POTTER FANS ONLY:
Answer: Dumbledore

Curious Kids Press
www.curiouskidspress.com

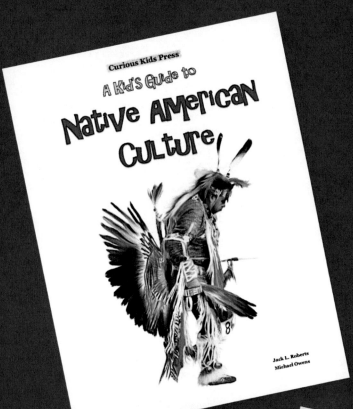

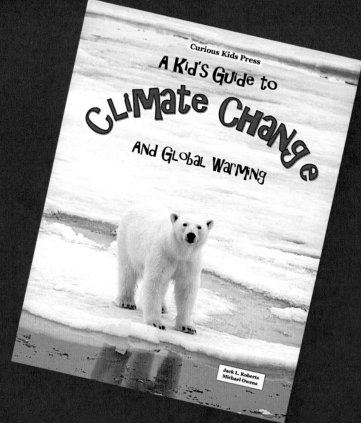

Two important new books for all young readers and their families.

Explore the World

Find these books on Amazon.com
Preview them at curiouskidspress.com

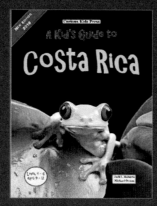

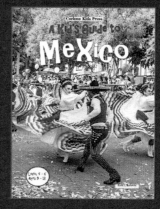
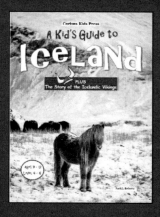
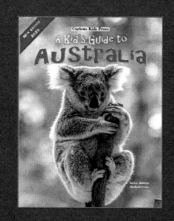

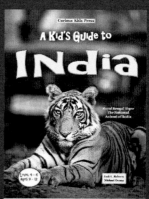

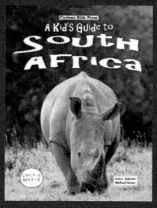

A Kid's Guide to
England
For Parents and Teachers

About This Book

A Kid's Guide to . . . is an engaging, easy-to-read book series that provides an exciting adventure into fascinating countries and cultures around the world for young readers. Each book focuses on one country, continent, or U.S. territory or state, and includes colorful photographs, informational charts and graphs, and quirky and bizarre "Did You Know" facts, all designed to bring the country and its people to life. Designed primarily for recreational, high-interest reading, the informational text series is also a great resource for students to use to research geography topics or writing assignments.

About the Reading Level

A Kid's Guide to . . . is an informational text series designed for kids in grades 4 to 6, ages 9 to 12. For some young readers, the series will provide new reading challenges based on the vocabulary and sentence structure. For other readers, the series will review and reinforce reading skills already achieved. While for still other readers, the book will match their current skill level, regardless of age or grade level.

About the Authors

Jack L. Roberts began his career in educational publishing at Children's Television Workshop (now Sesame Workshop), where he was Senior Editor of The Sesame Street/Electric Company Reading Kits. Later, at Scholastic Inc., he was the founding editor of a high-interest/low-reading level magazine for middle school students. He also founded two technology magazines for teachers and administrators.

Roberts is the author of more than two dozen biographies and other nonfiction titles for young readers, published by Scholastic Inc., the Lerner Publishing Group, Teacher Created Materials, Benchmark Education, and others.. More recently, he was the co-founder of WordTeasers, an educational series of card decks designed to help kids of all ages improve their vocabulary through "conversation, not memorization."

Michael Owens is a noted jazz dance teacher, award-winning wildlife photographer, graphic arts designer, and devoted animal lover.

In 2017, Roberts and Owens launched Curious Kids Press (CKP), an educational publishing company focused on publishing high-interest, nonfiction books for young readers, primarily books about countries and cultures around the world. Currently, CKP has published two series of country books: "A Kid's Guide to..." (for ages 9-12 and "Let's Visit . . ." (for ages 6-8) — both designed to help young readers explore the wonderful world of diversity in everything from food and holidays to geography and traditions.

To Our Valued Customers

Curious Kids Press is passionate about creating fun-to-read books about countries and cultures around the world for young readers, and we work hard every day to create quality products.

All of our books are Print on Demand books. As a result, on rare occasions, you may find minor printing errors. If you feel you have not received a quality printed product, please send us a description and photo of the printing error along with your name and address and we will have a new copy sent to you free of charge. Contact us at: info@curiouskidspress.com